One-Minute
Bible Stories
New Testament

Other books by Shari Lewis:
One-Minute Bedtime Stories
One-Minute Favorite Fairy Tales
One-Minute Animal Stories
One-Minute Bible Stories—Old Testament

One-Minute Bible Stories New Testament

Adapted by
Florence Henderson
and
Shari Lewis

Research by Gerry Matthews
Illustrated by C. S. Ewing

Doubleday

NEW YORK · LONDON · TORONTO · SYDNEY · AUCKLAND

The authors and the publisher gratefully acknowledge the assistance of D. Bruce Lockerbie and the reverend Chris Aridas in the preparation of this manuscript.

I'd like to dedicate this book to my future grandchildren, and to Matthew, Mark, Luke and John, without whom this project could never have come to pass.

Florence Henderson

Published by Doubleday
a division of Bantam Doubleday Dell Publishing Group, Inc.,
666 Fifth Avenue, New York, New York 10103

Doubleday and the portrayal of an anchor with a dolphin
are trademarks of Doubleday, a division of
Bantam Doubleday Dell Publishing Group, Inc.

Library of Congress Cataloging-in-Publication Data
Henderson, Florence.
  One-minute Bible stories, New Testament.
  Summary: Twenty Bible stories from the New Testament,
presented in a one-minute format, retell the life of Jesus.
  1. Bible stories, English—N.T.   [1. Bible stories—
N.T.]   I. Lewis, Shari.   II. Lewis, C. S., ill.   III. Title.
BS2401.H45   1986   225.9'505   86-6401

ISBN 0-385-23286-1 Trade
ISBN 0-385-23287-X Prebound

9 8 7 6 5 4

NIL

Contents

Introduction

As I put dictating machine to mouth (rather than pencil to paper—for when I write, I dictate my first version and then edit and augment for subsequent drafts), I found that adapting the Gospel was a very different endeavor from writing any of the previous One-Minute books. Instead of experiencing each story as a total (if tiny) happening, I got caught up in the flow of the action. Stripping each story down to its skeleton helped me to get an overview of the entire drama quickly. The unfolding of the tragedy moved me as it never has before.

Perhaps your youngsters will respond well to these one-minute New Testament stories for the same reason. Since the condensed versions are not bogged down with details, the lessons seem extra-clear to me. So does the inevitability of the behavior of each of the characters.

Obviously, one-minute Bible stories are not meant to take the place of religious education, but as a way to introduce or reinforce the tales, they provide an interesting supplement.

Now, considering how I feel about the one-minute tale, you can imagine how fascinated I was to read in an old issue of *Psychology Today* magazine (March 1982) that preschoolers and early graders are often overwhelmed by lengthy stories full of details. The article said, "Studies show that young children don't grasp motivation—what makes a character tick. They don't realize that characters change. Children tend to focus on surface features—what characters wear, own, want to have— more than on underlying motives and intentions—how they feel or what they seek. Surface details distract and even dominate a child's attention—however, when the plot is stripped down to bare essentials, so that all deceptive material has been eliminated, youngsters show more sensitivity to intention and motivation."

The article went on to deal with the value of repeated telling of tales, which is certainly more likely to happen if the story isn't long and tedious. (Tedious, that is, to the parent.)

In some homes, the New Testament is familiar material. My hope is that this book, containing the essence of each scriptural episode, will be read to or by every child who wouldn't otherwise be exposed to the stories of Jesus.

Whatever the specifics or intensity of your family's religious beliefs, I think the tales from the New Testament should be in every child's frame of reference. Not only are they exciting and touching stories, they are also undeniably a part of the foundation of all of our literary and cultural lives.

Shari Lewis

Mary and Joseph

Long ago, when Herod was king of Judea, a young woman named Mary was about to marry Joseph in the city of Nazareth. But before the wedding could take place, the angel Gabriel came down from heaven and told Mary that God was so pleased with her, He was going to give her a baby boy.

Surprised, Mary said, "How can I have a baby? I'm not even married yet."

"No matter," said Gabriel. "The Holy Spirit will put the baby in your womb, and when he is born he will be called the Son of God."

Mary worried, "What will Joseph think? Will he still want me for his wife?"

"I will tell Joseph," replied Gabriel, "and he will understand."

But when Joseph saw that Mary was going to have a baby, he was upset and decided to call off the wedding. After all, he knew the baby wasn't his.

But the angel told Joseph in a dream: "Don't be afraid to marry Mary. She has been chosen by the Lord to have His son. The child's name will be Jesus; he will be holy and will save the world from its sins."

So when Joseph woke up, he took Mary to the temple and married her. A little while later, they set out for Bethlehem.

The Birth of Jesus

Joseph took Mary to the town of Bethlehem to register their names with the government.

It was very cold, but when time came for Mary to have her baby there were no rooms left at the inn, so they took shelter in a stable, warmed only by the animals who slept there.

Joseph made Mary as comfortable as possible on the hay in the manger, and that night she gave birth to a baby boy. The animals crowded around to see the infant lying in the manger wrapped in his blanket.

Out in the fields, shepherds minding their sheep were stamping on the cold ground, trying to keep warm, when suddenly the sky lit up brighter than the sun. An angel of God

stood in front of them, saying, "I bring you wonderful news. Jesus Christ the Savior was born tonight. Go into Bethlehem and look for a baby lying in a manger." Then the heavens filled with lots of angels crying, "Glory to God and peace on earth!"

Amazed, the shepherds searched the barns and stables of Bethlehem until they found the little baby lying in the manger. The shepherds returned to the fields singing the praises of God, and telling everyone that Jesus Christ the Savior was born.

The Three Wise Men

After Jesus was born, three wise men traveled to Jerusalem in Israel, asking everyone, "Where is the baby Jesus, born to be king of the Jews? His star is in the east, and we want to bow before him and give him presents."

King Herod, afraid that this new king would take over *his* kingdom, told the wise men, "Find the baby, and then come back and tell me, so I can go worship him, too."

The wise men followed the star to Bethlehem and found Mary taking care of baby Jesus. They fell to their knees and offered presents of gold, incense, and stuff that smells good called myrrh.

An angel told them, "Herod intends to hurt the baby," so they didn't go back to Jerusalem as Herod had asked, but took a secret route to their own country. King Herod, furious to find he'd been tricked, ordered his soldiers to kill all boy babies in Bethlehem under the age of two, to make sure Jesus wouldn't grow up to be king.

That night an angel said to Joseph, "Take your family to Egypt, for Herod wants to kill the child." So they traveled to Egypt and stayed until the angel came again. "You can go home to Israel now," said the angel. "King Herod is dead."

Then Joseph took his family to Nazareth, where they could live in peace.

John the Baptist

Hundreds of years before the birth of Jesus, the prophet Isaiah predicted that a man would appear in the wilderness to prepare the world for the Lord's arrival. Jesus was about thirty when the prediction came true.

A man named John made great speeches to people who traveled to the wilderness from Jerusalem. He baptized them in the River Jordan and told them to confess their sins. He said, "He who has two coats, let him share with one who has none, and he who has food, let him do the same." Impressed, people thought John might be the one they'd been waiting for.

But John said, "There is another man, wiser and better

than I." He said, "I baptize you with water, but he'll baptize you with the Holy Spirit and fire. This man will separate the good from the bad."

Then Jesus came from Nazareth to be baptized by John. But John knew who he was and said, "You're asking me to baptize you? It is *you* who should baptize me!" But Jesus insisted, so John baptized him in the River Jordan. Then Jesus rose up out of the water, and the heavens opened wide. The spirit of God landed like a dove on his shoulder, and a voice from heaven said, "This is my Beloved Son, in whom I am well pleased."

Jesus Faces the Devil

After Jesus was baptized by John, God sent him into the wilderness. There, Jesus had nothing to eat for forty days and he was starving.

Suddenly the devil appeared and said, "If you're the Son of God, why don't you turn these stones into bread? Then you'll have plenty to eat." But Jesus wasn't fooled. "A man doesn't live on bread alone," he replied. "The word of God is just as important."

The devil didn't know what to say to that, so he put Jesus on the high roof of the temple—a dangerous place to be—saying, "Since you're the Son of God, jump off the roof and see if your Father catches you." Jesus smiled. "No—it's wrong to test God's love. You must have faith in Him."

Now the devil knew that if he could tempt Jesus, he could easily win over the rest of the people, so from the highest mountain peak he showed Jesus all the kingdoms of the world spread out below. "All these riches belong to me," he said. "Fall to your knees and worship me, and I will give you these beautiful kingdoms for your own."

"Go away, Satan!" ordered Jesus. "I will only worship the Lord my God, and Him alone will I serve."

Twelve Apostles

As Jesus traveled, his disciples followed him everywhere. He called twelve of these disciples "apostles" and gave them power to heal the sick, drive away evil spirits, and carry his teachings to all parts of the country.

There was Simon, whom Jesus renamed Peter, and his brother Andrew, and their fellow fishermen, the brothers James and John. Then came Philip, Bartholomew, Thomas, and another James. There was also Thaddeus, Matthew, and another known as Simon the patriot. And then there was Judas Iscariot, who would later become a traitor.

Jesus taught the apostles a new way of thinking: he told them that the poor were the most blessed people on earth because they would own the kingdom of God, that all who were hungry now would have plenty to eat, and the ones who were sad would find heaven a joyful place.

"Love your enemies," said Jesus, "and do good to people

who hate you. If someone hits you on the cheek, don't hit him back; offer him the other cheek instead. And if a robber takes your coat, offer him your shirt as well. Treat people the way *you* want to be treated. It's not up to you to decide who is right or wrong. Be kind, merciful, and forgiving to everyone. This is my gospel."

Two Fishes and Five Loaves of Bread

One day his disciples went up into the hills, followed by a crowd of five thousand people. Jesus was worried that they would go hungry.

He said to his disciple Philip, "How can we buy enough food to feed all those people?" Philip replied, "It would cost more money than I've ever *seen* to give each of them even a taste of food."

Andrew spotted a boy with two little fishes and five loaves of bread in his basket. "But," he said, "that wouldn't go very far in *this* crowd."

Jesus pointed to a field of grass nearby. "Have the people sit over there," he said.

Then he took the two fishes and five loaves of bread, thanked the Lord for them, and began handing them out to the hungry people. Each time the disciples reached into the basket, there were more fishes and plenty of bread and soon all five thousand had eaten their fill. And when they collected the leftovers there was still enough to fill twelve baskets.

Impressed by this miracle, the people said, "Jesus must be the true Christ who has come to us. We should make him our king!"

Jesus heard these words and slipped away by himself, because he didn't want to be king.

Walking on Water

Jesus wanted to be alone. He told his disciples to row their boat across the Sea of Galilee, and he would join them later on the other side.

He climbed into the hills to think and pray to God.

But when he got high up in the hills he looked out over the water and saw that the men were having trouble rowing against the wind. For every ten feet they rowed, the wind blew them back five. By dark they were only halfway across, and so tired they could hardly lift an oar.

Suddenly the disciple named Peter saw a figure walking across the water toward the boat. "What is that?" he whispered. "It's a man!" said another. "A man can't walk on water," gasped a third. "It must be a ghost." The figure came closer and said, "Don't be afraid. It is I, Jesus."

"Lord," said Peter. "If it is you, let me walk on the water too." Peter stepped out of the boat, walked on the water, and stood beside Jesus.

But then Peter looked down at the waves under his feet and was frightened. "I'm sinking!" he shouted. Immediately Jesus grasped Peter's hands and stopped him from sinking. "Oh, you of little faith," said Jesus. "Why do you doubt me?"

Jesus led Peter to the boat. The wind died down, and the disciples were able to row safely to shore.

The Good Samaritan

An expert on God's laws asked Jesus what he should do to go to heaven. "What do *you* think you should do?" Jesus responded. "I must love God with all my heart and strength, and love my neighbor as well," said the man. "You are right," Jesus replied. "But who is my neighbor?" the expert asked, and Jesus told this story:

"A traveler was beaten by robbers who left him half dead. A priest saw the bleeding man lying on the side of the road, but he turned his head the other way and went on by. Another passerby ignored the wounded traveler too, because he didn't want to be troubled. But when a man from Samaria saw what had happened, he tore his own robes to make bandages, poured medicine over the victim's wounds, lifted the man onto his donkey, and carried him to an inn. There he gave money to the innkeeper for room and food. 'Take care of this poor fellow until he is well enough to travel,' said the Samaritan. 'And if it costs more than I've given you, I promise to pay you back when I return this way.' "

Jesus then asked, "Which of these three men do *you* think was a neighbor to the traveler who was robbed and beaten?" The expert replied, "The one who gave him practical help." "Right," said Jesus. "Now you do the same for others."

Lazarus

Lazarus and his sisters Mary and Martha lived in the town of Bethany in Judea. Jesus was their friend. When Lazarus became really sick, Mary and Martha sent a message to Jesus (who was in another town preaching) asking for his help. Jesus said, "I will save Lazarus from death and show the power of the Son of God at the same time."

But Jesus' disciples begged him not to go. "The Pharisees

and high priests in Bethany think you are a fake, Master," they said. "They will stone you to death."

Jesus wouldn't listen. "This will give those who do not behave another chance."

Outside of Bethany, Mary and Martha and a crowd of mourners met Jesus and told him that Lazarus had died four days before and was already buried in a tomb.

"Show me where he is buried," said Jesus.

So they rolled the stone away from the door of the tomb. Jesus thanked God for being with him, and then to everyone's surprise shouted, "Lazarus, come out!" While everybody watched with wonder, the dead man appeared as alive and healthy as anybody.

Some of the mourners fell to their knees to worship Jesus but others were frightened and ran away to tell the Pharisees and the high priests what they'd seen.

The Plot

The Pharisees were religious men who were so strict they discouraged other people from believing in God. They heard Jesus claiming to be the Savior of all people, and were they upset! And when a lot of people began to believe in Jesus and follow his teachings instead of those of the Pharisees, they really became angry.

They complained to the priests, "Jesus performs miracles. He brought Lazarus back to life. If we let him continue, everyone will believe in him, and the Romans, who have the power of life and death over us, will destroy our whole nation."

The high priest Caiaphas agreed. "If Jesus dies, the people will come back to the old prophets."

So they plotted Jesus' death, and sent orders for anyone who knew where Jesus was to let them know, so they might arrest him.

Meanwhile, Jesus went to have dinner in Bethany with Lazarus, Mary, and Martha. At the table, Mary bathed his feet with a jar of expensive perfume and dried them with her hair.

The disciple Judas Iscariot said, "Why waste that valuable perfume? We could sell it and use the money to feed the poor." (Mind you, Judas didn't really care about the poor. He was a thief, and hoped to get the money for himself.)

But Jesus said, "Leave her be. She is saving this perfume to put on my body when I'm dead. You will always have the poor . . . you won't always have me."

The Final Journey

On the way to Jerusalem, Jesus gathered the twelve disciples around him. "When we reach the city," he said, "my enemies will arrest me and condemn me to death. They will torture me and nail me to a cross until I die. But three days later I will rise from the dead."

As they neared Jerusalem, crowds followed praising Jesus, and two blind men called out louder than the others, "Have mercy on us, Lord!"

Jesus stopped and asked them what they wanted. "Make us see again, Lord," said the blind men. Filled with pity, Jesus touched their eyes. Immediately they could see, and they joined the crowds going to Jerusalem.

On the outskirts of the city, Jesus told two of his disciples to search for a donkey tied to a fence. "Bring it here for me," he said. "And if anyone tries to stop you, tell them it is for the Lord."

The disciples brought the donkey back. They put their

coats on it as a saddle, and Jesus rode the donkey into Jerusalem.

Now the crowds ran ahead, shouting, "Blessed is he who comes in the name of the Lord!" The people in Jerusalem asked, "Who is this man?" And the crowds answered, "This is the prophet Jesus from the town of Nazareth. He is the Son of God."

The Last Supper

Alarmed at Jesus' popularity, the priests and the Pharisees got together with the high priest Caiaphas to discuss ways of capturing and killing Jesus without causing a riot amongst his followers.

But before they could think of a plan, the devil found his way into the disciple Judas Iscariot, who made Caiaphas an offer: "Give me thirty pieces of silver," said Judas, "and I'll hand Jesus over to you."

Of course, the high priest was delighted!

Now, on the day of the Passover feast, Jesus told Peter and John, "In the city, find a man carrying a jug of water. Follow him to a house and ask the master there in which room we may eat the Passover meal. He will show you a room with everything we need and *there* you must prepare the supper."

They did as Jesus said, and he sat with his disciples at the table. Jesus told them, "One of you is going to betray me."

They were upset, and each in turn said, "Lord, will it be me?" Jesus responded, "The one who is a traitor will wish he'd never been born."

Jesus passed around a loaf of bread, saying, "Eat this, it is my body." He poured wine and said, "Drink this, it is the blood I will shed to save the world from its sins." They ate the bread and drank the wine and Jesus said, "The next time we have wine together will be in God's heaven."

In the Garden of Gethsemane

After the Passover supper, Jesus walked with his disciples. "Tonight," he said, "you will all desert me."

Of course the disciples denied *that*. "Even if the others run away," said Peter, "I will stick by you."

Jesus replied, "Peter, before the rooster crows at dawn, you will swear three times that you don't know me." But Peter insisted, "I will stay with you, even if it means dying!"

At a garden at Gethsemane, Jesus told the disciples to wait while he went a little distance away to pray. Peter, John, and James saw him trembling. "I am troubled because of what is about to happen," he said. "Keep watch over me."

34

Jesus prayed, "Father, if possible, please don't make me go through this terrible thing. I'll do it if that's what you want, but I'd rather not, if there's any way out."

Then Jesus saw that the three who were supposed to be watching him were asleep. He suggested to them, "Perhaps if you pray, you can resist the temptation to sleep." He went away and prayed again for God to make him able to bear the suffering he would soon face. When he returned, the three disciples were still asleep. He prayed a third time and then awakened them.

"Watch now and you will see the Son of God captured by sinners," he said. "The time has come. Look! Here they are!"

The Kiss of Death

Men with swords and clubs surrounded Jesus and his disciples. Judas Iscariot went up to Jesus and kissed him so the men would know whom to capture.

When they grabbed Jesus, Peter pulled out his sword, but Jesus said, "Don't show your sword unless you are ready to die by it. Besides, don't you know that I could ask my Father to send down an army of angels to protect me?"

He asked the armed men, "Why have you come after me *now*, as if I were a robber? You've seen me sitting in the temple every day and you didn't arrest me then. You are doing exactly as I knew you would."

All the disciples ran away except Peter, who watched from a distance as the men dragged Jesus to the high priest Caiaphas. The priests tried to prove Jesus guilty, but of course they couldn't.

At last Caiaphas demanded, "Are you Jesus Christ, the Son of God?" Jesus replied, "You have said it."

The furious priests shouted, "For that, you will die!"

A woman saw Peter watching and said, "He's one of the disciples!" But Peter protested, "You're wrong, woman. I never saw him before." Then a man pointed and said, "You *are* one of them." Again Peter denied it. Finally a third person insisted, "That man is Jesus' friend." When Peter shook his head he heard the rooster crow and he wept, for he knew Jesus' prophecy had come true.

Pontius Pilate

Declared guilty by Caiaphas, Jesus was taken to the palace of Pontius Pilate, the Roman governor of Judea.

Pilate asked, "Has this man broken the law?"

The priests replied, "Would we bring him to you if he weren't guilty?"

"Then *you* punish him," said Pilate.

"It is against our religion to kill a man," they answered.

So the governor asked Jesus, "Are you really the king of the Jews, as they say you are?"

Jesus responded, "My kingdom is not on earth but in heaven."

"So you *are* a king, then?" asked Pilate.

"That's what *you* say," said Jesus. "*I* say that I was put on earth to teach the truth. Anyone who loves truth will listen to me."

Pilate told the crowd he believed Jesus was innocent of any crime. But they shouted, "Kill him!", so to avoid a riot Pilate had his soldiers whip Jesus and beat him with a stick. They put a crown of thorns on his head and then Pilate showed Jesus to the crowd, saying, "See? I *have* punished him, but I still can't find any reason to put him to death." "He must die," demanded the priests. "He says he is the Son of God, and that is a serious crime."

So the priests got the Roman soldiers to take Jesus to his death.

The Crucifixion

When Pontius Pilate gave Jesus back to his enemies, they made him and two robbers each carry a big wooden cross through the streets of Jerusalem. Then they nailed all three to their crosses. As the soldiers drove the nails in, Jesus said, "Forgive them, Father; they don't understand what they are doing."

The soldiers raised the crosses and stood them in a row, Jesus in the middle with a sign over his head that read, "This is the king of the Jews."

The priests and the Pharisees shouted, "If he is the Son of God, why doesn't his Father save him now?" And the soldiers called, "Hey, king of the Jews, you're good at miracles—let's see you get down off that cross!"

Even one of the robbers, suffering as he was, joined in, but the second robber said, "Leave him alone. You and I deserve to be punished, but this man has done nothing wrong." Then he said to Jesus, "Remember me when you reach your kingdom, Lord."

In spite of his misery, Jesus replied, "The truth is, you will be in paradise with me this very day."

Suddenly the sky grew dark as if a storm were about to break. Jesus cried out, "Father! I commit my spirit into your hands!" And then he died.

41

The Tomb

When Jesus died on the cross, the ground shook, rocks split in two, and graves opened as the bodies of the dead rose and walked through Jerusalem. People were frightened and a soldier said, "Truly, he *was* the Son of God."

Later that evening, a loyal disciple of Jesus' named Joseph got Pontius Pilate's permission to remove the body from the cross and prepare it for burial.

Joseph carefully wrapped Jesus in new linen cloth and carried him to his *own* tomb, which had been carved into the side of a stone hill. There he laid the body down and rolled a heavy boulder over the entrance, so no one could get in. Women who had followed Jesus in his travels gathered nearby to mourn his death.

Next morning the priests and the Pharisees went to Pi-

late and told him: "Jesus said he would rise from the dead in three days. We think the tomb should be guarded by soldiers so his disciples don't come in the dark of night, steal the body, and claim that by some miracle Jesus has come back to life. That would make people believe Jesus' lies about being the Son of God."

So Pilate posted two soldiers at the tomb with instructions to keep everyone away until after the third day.

The Resurrection

On the third day after Jesus was crucified, as Mary Magdalene and another loyal female follower approached the tomb, there was an earthquake and an angel of God came down from heaven and rolled the boulder away from the door of the tomb.

The angel sat on the rock, glowing like lightning. The soldiers guarding the door were so frightened, they fainted. The angel told the women not to be afraid. "You are looking for Jesus who was crucified but he isn't here. He has risen from the dead, as he said he would."

The angel showed the women that the open tomb was empty except for the linen cloth that had been wrapped around the body. "Go quickly," said the angel, "tell his disciples what you have seen. Tell them also that Jesus will visit them soon."

The angel went back to heaven, and the women ran to tell the disciples the news. Suddenly Jesus himself stepped in front of them. The women fell to their knees. Jesus repeated what the angel had said and asked the women to hurry. Meanwhile the guards at the tomb woke up from their faint and ran to the temple to let the priests know what had happened.

The priests gave the soldiers money and made them promise to keep it a secret. "Instead," they said, "tell everyone that his disciples stole the body while you were asleep. Don't let the people find out what really happened or they will worship Jesus forever."

Jesus Goes to Heaven

When Mary Magdalene told the disciples about Jesus rising from the dead, they thought she was making it up. So Peter and John went to see for themselves. They found the tomb open and the body gone. John now believed, but Peter wasn't sure what it all meant. That night, the disciples met secretly and locked the door so they wouldn't be found by the priests and Pharisees and killed like Jesus. They talked of the strange and awful things that had happened and wondered what to do.

Suddenly Jesus was there, and they all trembled, thinking he was a ghost. Jesus said, "Why can't you believe I'm really here? Look at the holes the nails made in my hands and feet. Touch me. Ghosts don't have warm skin, as I do. I told you many times that I would be arrested, beaten, crucified, and that on the third day I would rise again and walk with you. And I have taught you that love and forgiveness should be preached to

the people of the world. Now it is up to you to spread the word."

Jesus blessed his disciples, and then he went up to heaven.

With joy in their hearts, the disciples returned to Jerusalem to pray in the temple and thank God for letting them know Jesus.

Florence Henderson, the youngest of ten children, was born in Dale, Indiana, to a close-knit family short on money but long on love. Though she received no formal musical training until she was seventeen, Florence could sing fifty songs by the time she was two. Soon after studying at New York's rigorous Academy of Dramatic Arts, she was invited to play the role of the heroine in Rodgers and Hammerstein's *Oklahoma,* and later played the lead role of Maria in *The Sound of Music.* Florence went on to head her own situation-comedy series, "The Brady Bunch," in which she courageously played the mother of six children. Quietly and unassumingly, Florence Henderson has become a top star. She's definitely a lady to watch . . . and listen to . . . and applaud.

World-famous ventriloquist and puppeteer **Shari Lewis** (also known as Lamb Chop's mother) has been honored with five Emmy Awards, a Peabody, the Monte Carlo TV Award for World's Best Variety Show, and the 1983 Kennedy Center Award for Excellence and Creativity in the Arts; she is presently Chairman of the Board of Trustees of the International Reading Foundation. One of the few female symphony conductors, she has performed with and conducted more than 100 symphony orchestras, including the National Symphony at Kennedy Center, the Pittsburgh Symphony, the National Arts Centre Orchestra of Canada, and the Osaka National Symphony in Japan.

Besides the recently published *One-Minute Animal Stories,* Shari Lewis is the author of *One-Minute Bedtime Stories* and *One-Minute Favorite Fairy Tales* for Doubleday, both juvenile bestsellers. *One-Minute Bible Stories,* both Old and New Testament, are available as Magic Window home video cassettes.

C. S. Ewing is an illustrator of works for children that include books, textbooks, and magazine stories. She studied at the Art Institute in Kansas City, Missouri, the city where she now lives and works.